Get Well Soon!

I Have a
Cold

Gillian Gosman

PowerKiDS press.

New York

Published in 2013 by The Rosen Publishing Group, Inc.
29 East 21st Street, New York, NY 10010

First Edition

Editor: Jennifer Way
Book Design: Greg Tucker
Layout Design: Kate Laczynski

Photo Credits: Cover Wavebreak Media/Thinkstock; p. 4 Jose Luis Pelaez Inc/Blend Images/Getty Images; p. 5 (top) Tom Le Groff/Digital Vision/Thinkstock; p 5 (bottom) ZenShui/Odilon Dimier/PhotoAlto Agency RF Collections/Getty Images; pp. 6, 12, 19 (top), 20 Shutterstock.com; p. 7 Mark Giles/Photo Researchers/Getty Images; p. 8 Dr. Gopal Murti/Visuals Unlimited/Getty Images; p. 9 Adrian Pope/Photographer's Choice/Getty Images; p. 10 Tom Merton/OJO Images/Getty Images; p. 11 © www.iStockphoto.com/Nathan Maxfield; pp. 13, 14–15 JGI/Jamie Grill/Blend Images/Getty Images; p. 16 Aaron Haupt/Photo Researchers/Getty Images; p. 17 © www.iStockphoto.com/Mlenny Photography; p. 18 Creatas Images/Creatas/Thinkstock; p. 19 (bottom) Spencer Platt/Staff/Getty Images News/Getty Images; p. 21 © www.iStockphoto.com/Bonnie Jacobs; p. 22 Tom Le Goff/Photodisc/Thinkstock.

Library of Congress Cataloging-in-Publication Data

Gosman, Gillian.
I have a cold / by Gillian Gosman. — 1st ed.
   p. cm. — (Get well soon!)
Includes index.
ISBN 978-1-4488-7408-8 (library binding)
1. Cold (Disease)—Juvenile literature. I. Title.
RF361.G68 2013
616.2'05—dc23
                              2011046908

Manufactured in the United States of America

CPSIA Compliance Information: Batch #SW12PK: For Further Information contact Rosen Publishing, New York, New York at 1-800-237-9932

Contents

I Have a Cold

People with colds often have stuffy or runny noses. ▼

If you are like most kids, you have had a cold. You could not stop coughing. Your throat and head might have hurt. Your nose was stuffed up. You also may have had a fever, or a raised body temperature. You probably did not want to eat. You just wanted to stay in bed all day.

Did you wonder how you got that cold and what was

When you are coming down with a cold, you may feel tired all day. ▶

It is a good idea to take your temperature with a thermometer to see if you have a fever. ▶

happening inside your body as it worked to get well again? This book will tell you what is going on in your body when you have a cold.

5

What Is a Cold?

Being outside in cold weather will not cause you to catch a cold. This is one of the many incorrect things some people believe about the common cold. ▼

The common cold is an **infection** of the upper **respiratory system**. The respiratory system includes the passageways of the throat and nose. Some kids can get eight colds every year, each cold lasting as long as a week. Colds are most common during cold weather. This may be because when the weather is cold, people stay indoors. This makes it easier for people to share the **germs** that cause colds.

6

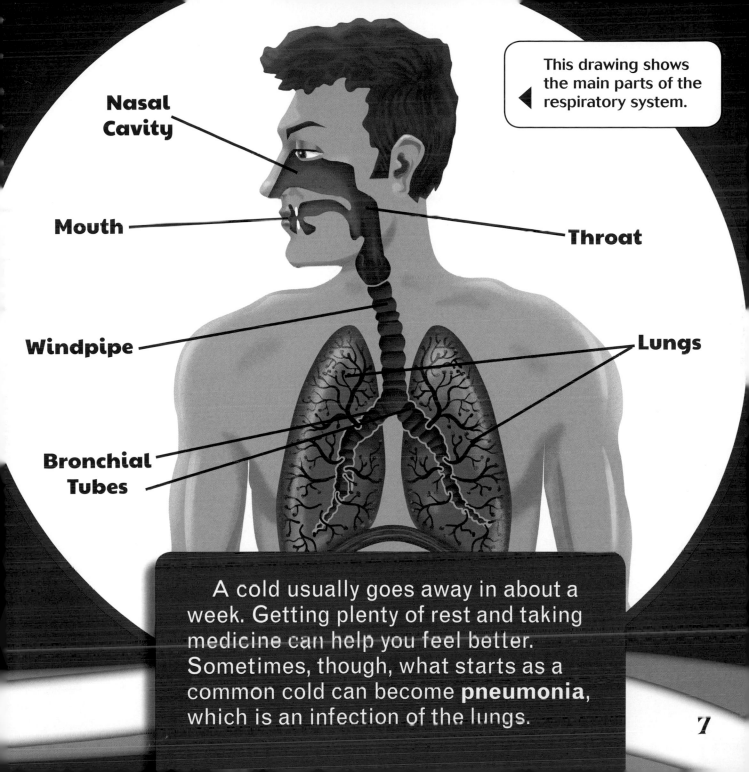

Nasal Cavity

Mouth

Windpipe

Bronchial Tubes

Throat

Lungs

This drawing shows the main parts of the respiratory system.

A cold usually goes away in about a week. Getting plenty of rest and taking medicine can help you feel better. Sometimes, though, what starts as a common cold can become **pneumonia**, which is an infection of the lungs.

7

What Causes a Cold?

A **virus** causes the common cold. There are more than 200 different viruses that cause colds. They all leave you feeling under the weather, though!

A virus is a tiny thing, too small to be seen by your eyes alone. A virus needs living **cells** to host, or

These blue blobs are one example of the hundreds of different kinds of viruses that can cause colds. Viruses are so small they can be seen only with very powerful microscopes.

Blowing your nose helps clear a runny or stuffy nose. You might feel like your nose is going to be stuffy forever, but it will usually clear up after a few days. ▼

support it. It cannot be on its own. The human body is a great host for the cold virus. Viruses want to stay and take over. Our bodies work hard to get rid of viruses, though.

Body aches and chills are cold symptoms you can tell a parent, nurse, or doctor about. This helps her figure out what is wrong so that she can make you feel more comfortable. ▼

The signs and **symptoms** of the common cold are clear. A sign is a medical term that describes information a doctor can gather by looking or using medical tools. A symptom is a medical term that describes information the patient gives based on what he is feeling.

Doctors will take note of signs such as a fever and swollen, or larger than normal, **glands**. The patient will tell the doctor about symptoms such as a runny nose, a sore throat, body aches, and a headache.

Doctors listen to your breathing and coughing when you have a respiratory sickness like a cold. They are looking for signs that tell them whether you have a cold or another illness. ▶

What's Going On in My Body?

Once a cold virus enters your body, it is on the lookout for a healthy cell. It forces this host cell to create copies of the virus until the host cell is so big that it bursts. This releases the virus, which then spreads, attacking other healthy cells. That is when your body's **immune system** fights back.

◀ A cool washcloth on your forehead can make you feel a little better when you have a fever.

You get rid of mucus when you blow your nose. You also let out small droplets of mucus when you cough or sneeze.

▼

It sends virus-fighting cells to destroy the virus. These cells can cause **inflammation**, which can lead to a fever. Your immune system also makes a lot of yucky green and yellow **mucus** to trap the virus.

How Did I Catch a Cold?

Viruses travel through the air in tiny drops of mucus. This is the liquid inside your respiratory system. If a healthy person breathes in these tiny drops of liquid, he can get sick. If the liquid lands on a hard surface, a healthy person can become sick by touching the surface and then touching his mouth, eyes, or nose.

Just 12 hours after the virus first enters your body, it has made copies of itself and attacked healthy cells. This is when your immune system begins to fight back and the signs and symptoms begin to appear.

Cold viruses spread easily. This is why family members often suffer from colds at the same time. Covering your mouth when you sneeze or cough can help keep germs from spreading, though.

Going to the Doctor

Most colds can be treated with rest and over-the-counter medicines that relieve symptoms. ▼

Doctors say that people should visit their doctors if their fever goes above 103° F (39° C), if they throw up or have stomach pain, if they have trouble breathing, or if their ears hurt. These signs and symptoms tell doctors that a patient may have a more serious sickness than a cold. For these symptoms, doctors may **prescribe**

> You should visit a doctor if you do not feel like you are getting better after over a week. You may have something more serious than a cold.

powerful medicines. If you are generally healthy and do not have these signs and symptoms, you likely do not need to visit a doctor. Most colds run their course on their own. Your immune system fights the virus and wins!

How a Cold Is Treated

To help your immune system do its work, one of the best things you can do is to drink plenty of water. You should also get plenty of rest. Taking an over-the-counter painkiller will help lower your temperature and ease your achy muscles.

Many people like to eat chicken soup when they have a cold. Any hot soup you like can help soothe your sore throat, though. ▶

Over-the-counter painkillers and cough medicines do not kill the cold virus, but they help relieve fevers and coughing. ▶

Children's **TYLENOL** *Plus* COLD

Concentrated **TYLENOL** INFANTS' DROPS
Fever Reducer, Pain Reliever, Nasal Decongestant
Plus COLD
CONTAINS 2 INGREDIENTS:
• Fever & Pain
• Stuffy Nose
Phenylephrine HCl
NEW Dosing Device
BUBBLE GUM FLAVOR   USE ONLY Enclosed Syringe
New Decongestant See New Dosing
1/2 FL OZ (15mL)

Concentra. **TYLENOL** *Plus* COLD
NDC 50580-393-15
Fever Reducer, Pain Reliever, Nasal Decongestant, Antihistamine
CONTAINS 3 INGREDIENTS:
• Fever & Sore Throat
Acetaminophen
• Stuffy Nose
Phenylephrine HCl
• Sneezing & Runny Nose
Chlorpheniramine Maleate
New Decongestant See New Dosing
GRAPE FLAVOR
4 FL OZ (120mL)

Concentra. **TYLENOL** INFANTS' DROPS
Fever Reducer, Pain Reliever, Nasal Decongestant, Cough Suppressant
Plus COLD & COUGH
CONTAINS 3 INGREDIENTS:
• Fever & Pain
Acetaminophen
• Stuffy Nose
Phenylephrine HCl
• Cough
Dextromethorphan HBr
NEW Dosing Device
CHERRY FLAVOR
ORAL SUSPENSION
New Decongestant See New Dosing

◀ You should take only the children's formula of over-the-counter medicines. They should be given only by an adult and taken following the directions on the package.

While you have a cold, you should try to avoid being in crowded places. That is because you are **contagious**. This means you are able to pass your cold on to someone else. You are also more likely to catch another sickness when your immune system is busy fighting your cold.

How to Prevent a Cold

The common cold is easily passed from person to person. The best way to avoid getting sick is to limit the amount of time you spend with people sick with a cold.

If you do come into contact with a sniffling, sneezing, and coughing friend, try to avoid her germs. Wash your hands. Do not share food or drinks. Try to avoid touching

▲
Washing your hands with soap and water is one of the easiest ways you can avoid catching or spreading germs.

Colds can spread easily at school, ▶ where people spend a lot of time together indoors. That is why it is important to learn about ways to keep germs from spreading.

your eyes, nose, or mouth. Clean household and school surfaces with **disinfecting** spray or wipes. Finally, keep your immune system strong by eating healthy foods, exercising, and taking good care of yourself.

The Road to Recovery

Taking good care of yourself when you have a cold will help you get better quickly. Hot drinks can help clear your stuffy nose and make a sore throat feel better.
▼

Within hours of the cold virus entering your body, you will start to feel the first symptoms. You are contagious for the next two to four days. Generally, you will get better quickly and completely. If the cold leads to an ear infection or pneumonia, though, and this sickness is not treated, more serious problems may follow.

Chances are you will catch at least one cold each year. If you do, now you know what to expect and how to take better care of yourself.

22

Glossary

cells (SELZ) The basic units of living things.

contagious (kun-TAY-jus) Able to pass a sickness on.

disinfecting (dis-in-FEKT-ing) Making something clean and free of things that can make people sick.

germs (JERMZ) Tiny living things that can cause sickness.

glands (GLANDZ) Organs or body parts that produce elements to help with bodily functions.

immune system (ih-MYOON SIS-tem) The system that keeps the body safe from sicknesses.

infection (in-FEK-shun) A sickness caused by germs.

inflammation (in-fluh-MAY-shun) Something that is sore or swollen.

mucus (MYOO-kus) Thick, slimy matter produced by the body.

pneumonia (noo-MOH-nya) An illness that people can get in their lungs.

prescribe (prih-SKRYB) To order a certain kind of medicine.

respiratory system (RES-puh-ruh-tawr-ee SIS-tem) The parts of the body that help in breathing.

symptoms (SIMP-tumz) Signs that show people are sick.

virus (VY-rus) Something tiny that causes a disease.

Index

Websites

Due to the changing nature of Internet links, PowerKids Press has developed an online list of websites related to the subject of this book. This site is updated regularly. Please use this link to access the list: www.powerkidslinks.com/gws/cold/